A Prophecy For a King

Bryan A. Helsby

First edition 2004
Published by The Brenin Project

ISBN:
0-9549456-0-3

Copyright © Bryan A Helsby 2004

The right of Bryan A Helsby to be identified as the author of this work has been asserted by him in accordance with the copyright, Designs and Patents Act 1988.

All rights reserved. No reproduction, copy or transmission of this publication may be made without written permission. No paragraph of this publication may be reproduced, copied or transmitted save with written permission or in accordance with the provisions of the Copyright Act 1956 (as amended). Any person who does any unauthorised act in relation to this publication may be liable to criminal prosecution and civil claims for damages.

Printed by Gomer Press, Llandysul, Ceredigion.

This book is sold subject to the condition that it shall not by way of trade or otherwise, be lent, re-sold, hired out or otherwise circulated without the publisher's prior consent in any form of binding or cover other than that in which it is published and without a similar condition including this condition being imposed on the subsequent purchaser.

Y Mab Darogan
"The Son Foretold"

During the 7th century the famous Druid, named Myrddyn (Merlin), foretold of a great son who would deliver his people from the Saxon oppressor and once more possess the land of their ancestors.

This foretelling of such a son would ring throughout the centuries inspiring generations of leaders whose valiant efforts would give rise to a nation's birth.

Cymru (Wales), however, would struggle to survive against a succession of ruthless invaders but such words always kept hope alive. Words sung by the Bards in the 'long yellow summer' of 1485 as Henry Tudor fulfilled this destiny to claim the throne of England, the King born of an ancient Prophecy...

A Prophecy for a King

Introduction

A Prophecy for a King is a timeless account of a people's struggle to win independence and of words spoken by Druidic Prophets that told of a great leader, a Celtic King who would unite the ancient Kingdoms and drive out all invaders.

These words would live to inspire generations for centuries to come, even during the darkest days when all seemed lost and in so doing, this Prophecy charts the bloodlines of Welsh princes who fought against a succession of English Kings ambitious to forge their mighty realms. Leaders whose efforts become woven into a nation's struggle to grow and a people's desire for recognition.

All would heed this Prophecy throughout the most evocative periods of Wales' history and those who listened would influence the shaping of the world.

Prologue

In the war of 1282 with Prince Llywelyn's tragic death and the brutal execution of his brother, Dafydd, the male line from Gwynedd, whose ancestors had striven for centuries to build and retain a nation, had finally come to an end. Not since Roman times had such a military occupation been seen but, unlike then, King Edward I completed the task by dissecting the land into English governed counties and surrounded Wales with mighty stone castles to enforce their rule.

But the Celtic Bards continued to sing of the ancient prophecies that a great leader would yet restore their land and gain power over England which had been lost with the coming of the Saxons.

With such voices at least hope could be kept alive, for to even challenge English domination would take a very special leader possessing the qualities of all the great names from the past, one whom the Bards would sing of as, 'The Rise of Owain Glyndŵr.'

On the sixteenth day of September in the year 1400 a secret meeting took place in the beautiful Dee Valley, near Corwen, whereby the title of 'Prince of Wales,' not heard since the heady days of Prince Llywelyn over a century before, was bestowed upon and excepted by a man directly descended from the Princes of Powys and peppered with the genes of Llywelyn's descendents. By so doing, Owain Glyndŵr and his small band of supporters had begun Wales' final and most bitter war for independence. A war that would shake the English throne to its very foundations.

Within five years control of virtually all Wales lay in Welsh hands. The newly captured Harlech Castle becomes Owain's Head Quarters and a Parliament is seated in Machynlleth where he produces his own chancery and seals. Two universities are sited, one in the north and one in the south, to educate those needed to administer a country.

The long and bloody struggle against all odds had been won. However, this tenuous hold had yet to be consolidated.

Meanwhile the Marcher Lord, Edmund Mortimer, held hostage by Owain and whose claim to the English throne rivalled the King's, moved over to the Welsh cause and marries Owain's daughter, Catherine. This alliance plus support from the powerful Percys of Northumberland creates an audacious and ambitious plan.

By 1405 this pact is sealed with the signing of the Tripartite Indenture which would give Owain Wales and a large tract of western England, the Percys the whole of the north and Mortimer the south east of England.

If they could defeat King Henry.

However, in this same year English dominance begins to reassert itself. The political situation in Scotland no longer posed a threat, and with Ireland now suppressed, Wales would soon stand alone.

Yet the struggle begins, not with Owain Glyndŵr, rather over a thousand years before when the Roman Empire ruled the World and Pagan Druids prophesied of a Celtic King….

The Coming Of the Saxons

In the year of our Lord, 51 AD, the might of the Roman Empire turned on Briton. This mosaic of warring Celtic tribes would prove no match for Rome's relentless Legions and within 10 years the invaders' grip stretched into the far north and reached into the wild, mountainous lands of the west.

The Celts still resisted for they possessed a powerful bond; a religion of fire, earth, water and wind deeply engraved into their souls, but the Roman Governor General, Sutoneous Paulinous, had plans to strike at their very heart.

In the year 60 AD the island of Ynys Mon, 'The Mother Isle,' (Anglesey) fell victim to his ruthless efficiency for here lay the centre of the Druids' power, here priests studied alongside scholars of history and wizards practised their art. From Ynys Mon radiated the Celts' religion. In the ensuing attack few escaped the slaughter, fleeing the smoking pyres as their sacred oak groves burned, never to re-grow.

As the Legionnaires rested from their work word reached the Governor General of a massive Celtic uprising in the south. The harsh injustices of Roman rule drove Boudica and a coalition of tribes into a killing frenzy and determination to rid Briton of the invaders once and for all.

The Legionnaires received orders to march and in a shallow vale in the southern Midlands formed the battle lines that destroyed an army over six times their number.

Briton had become Roman.

In the wild lands of the west, where the Celts still proved troublesome, the Legions concentrated on protecting the supply routes and coastal regions along which copper, tin and gold flowed eastward to feed the voracious appetite of the Roman Empire.

Then, as the centuries passed, Celtic culture began to fade into a dim light only a few could still see. This small band passed on their beliefs generation after generation trying to maintain by word of mouth, by story and epic poem, the Druidic culture only spoken, never written.

Not until the year 408 AD when communication with Rome is threatened by an invasion of barbarians across the Rhine are orders issued to abandon this colony on the edge of the habitable world and withdraw to Gaul.

The coming of the Saxons was about to change everything as they pushed the mighty Romans deep into southern Europe then looked west to the rich island colony abandoned by Rome.

In the year 410 AD the Roman Emperor, Honorious instructs the cities of Briton, 'Look to your own defences.'

The Saxons were coming but this would be no grand invasion as seen nearly four centuries ago but an incoming tide of immigrants hungry for land and willing to battle for it.

A Celtic revival was also taking place including old tribal rivalries but against the relentless Saxon expansion from the east resistance proved only temporary. The Celts were cast as second class citizens as the birth of a new country took place. Ingland, from Hadrian's Wall to the south coast channel. Only three regions in the west continued to resist then Cumbria, followed by Cornwall, fell until only the wild regions of western Briton remained truly Celtic. They called themselves the 'Gymru,' the Patriots.

Tribal differences were put aside in the face of a common enemy while the Druid culture began to reassert itself and speak of a great leader, 'he will come down from the mountains as a two edged sword,' Mab y Darogan, a promised King who would fulfil the prophecy of Myrddyn, 'Merlin,' and deliver his people from the hated Saxon oppressor and return control of Briton to the Celts.

Many believed Arthur to be the chosen King. A warrior chieftain able to unite the tribes and defeat the Saxon in battle, but this would not be so, though he would remain forever as a symbol of hope and grant the words of a prophecy with immortality.

As the Saxons pressed ever westward a smaller migration of Celts from north of Hadrian's Wall trying to flee Saxon rule would prove of much greater influence. The Votoclini, led by Cunnedda Wledig and accompanied by his eight sons and one grandson sail down the coast from the Firth of the Forth to land at Ynys Mon and establish themselves at Aberffraw.

A dynasty is founded which soon expands onto the mainland but not until Cunnedda's great grandson, Maelgwyn Gwynedd, do they consolidate their hold. He increases the territory and names this hard won kingdom after himself, Gwynedd. A name that would survive the centuries and give rise to a host of leaders.

Meanwhile the constant power struggle in Ingland gradually develops into three main regions. The northern Saxons rule Northumbria, middle Saxons rule Mercia and western Saxons rule Wessex in the south west. These three kingdoms all possess an open frontier to the Celtic west offering followers better prospects of land and treasure but are plagued by civil war and assassination yet still they find the energy to drive the Celts further back.

Then, amidst the violence, Saints begin to roam the land spreading the Christian influence. Against the new, all powerful God the Pagan Druids cannot compete. Having withstood the might of Rome their power now begins to wane but the deep rooted traditions of poetry and fine speech would survive and these words would take with them the prophesy for a Celtic king.

In Ingland the Mercian's finally achieve military superiority over the other Saxons and in turn now constitute a very serious threat to Gwynedd where the Celtic shield walls hold against the mighty Mercian's but the raids grew more frequent and run ever deeper.

King Offa of Mercia consolidates his power and in display of his standing issues the first significant Royal coinage. He also organises the building of Offa's Dyke, an immense earthwork system stretching from the Dee estuary in the north to the mouth of the Wye in the south, creating the first recognisable political boundary between Saxon Ingland and the Celtic kingdoms in the west. In so doing he unwittingly mapped the future of two nations.

Briton was about to undergo a major transition as the Wessex Saxons, led by Egbert, take full advantage of King Offa's death in 796 AD and go onto receive homage from all the Saxons thereby creating a unified England and in the west a new ruler of Gwynedd, Merfyn Frych, begins a political union of the Celtic Kingdoms.

Merfyn rules a cosmopolitan and literate court. He marries Nest, sister of Cyngen, ruler of Powys, and they produce a son they name Rhodri.

People ask, 'could this be the heir to fulfil the prophesy?' and hoped.

Certainly the son, like his father, encouraged the collecting and writing down of the lore, until now passed on only by the spoken word by storytellers and poets; Bards who continued the ancient practice around winter fires to enraptured audiences who listened to tales of a great leader yet to emerge and win, against seemingly impossible odds.

In 844 AD Rhodri succeeds his father and the unification of Celtic Kingdoms into a country begins, named Gymru in their own tongue, a country that would become known as Wales to all others.

Eleven years on the King of Powys, Cyngen, dies whilst on a pilgrimage to Rome leaving his kingdom to Rhodri who also inherits the violent feud along the Saxon border, Offa's Dyke. He becomes the first ruler of both states then marries Angharad, sister of Gwgon, ruler of Ceredigion, who bears him six sons and so continues his father's policy by uniting without striking a blow.

Rhodri's rule, however, would not prove strife free for the threat would not only come from the east but from the west as a new enemy began to strike terror into the heart of his newly formed nation.

From the fjords of Scandinavia two growing powers, the Danes and the Norwegians, sail forth in their long boats seeking treasure, slaves and glory in battle.

In Europe Emperor Charlemagne dies and as his Empire crumbles these Norsemen seize the opportunity to attack while continuing to press parts of England, Scotland and then Ireland. This western outpost of Celtic culture had escaped Roman rule and Saxon invasion but by 853 AD, after an overwhelming victory, the Norsemen become Lords of Ireland and prepare to unleash their full force on Wales.

Ynys Mon is devastated but after Rhodri kills the Danish leader, Horm, in a sea battle, he foils their attempt to gain a permanent foothold.

Rhodri maintains a well ordered government and concentrates on creating a united Wales defending its borders with valiant efforts in battle and is awarded the additional name, Mawr (the Great), but he showed no sign of hurling the Saxons back into the sea.

In 877 AD he dies defending his realm which is divided amongst the three strongest sons thereby accounting for the Celtic tradition known as gavel kind.

Rhodri had taken a collection of small states, led by proud, independent princes, and died leaving a united realm. However, the cracks soon begin to reappear.

England would not fare so well.

In 865 AD three hundred long boats land on the Northumbrian coast and the great army strikes inland swiftly reducing virtually all of England to a sword land ruled by Viking warriors. Wessex alone survives and under the rule of its new ruler, King Alfred, becomes the focus of Saxon resistance. Fortresses or 'Burghs,' are built to ward off future attacks and he orders a great fleet of warships to be built countering the long boats. Then he turns to the heavy task of regaining the rest of England. For his many achievements Alfred is awarded the title of, 'The Great,' but the Vikings would prove formidable opponents.

Viking settlements in the north swell with an influx of migrating colonists and, as in Ireland, cultures and marriages merge. By the year 911 AD the persistent raids on the continent drive the King of France, Charles the Simple, to give permission to a powerful band of these Norsemen to settle on France's northwest coast. Their leader, a Christian named Rollo, calls this settlement, Normandy (North man's Land) and from these meagre beginnings would rise a fearful force.

Meanwhile the Viking attacks on Wales are about to begin with renewed ferocity.

To counter these 'Black Foreigners' another great leader must emerge and Rhodri's grandson, Hywel, would prove the strongest but realises he must make a pact with the hated Saxon to concentrate on the Viking threat. He also sets in motion many changes including regulations to produce a unified law, requiring proof of guilt rather than trial by ordeal.

Hywel proves himself a gifted politician and man of peace for which he receives the title of, Dda, 'The Good,' but his death leaves a period of confusion and internal conflict.

The Vikings take full advantage.

In the raids on Ynys Mon one thousand defenders perish and two thousand are carried off as captives while in South Wales St David's is ransacked four times and in the last raid of 999 AD the Bishop of Morganeau is murdered. The raids also extend to south east England and London where the prize at stake is nothing less than the throne itself.

The millennium dawns on bleak hopes although new leaders emerge from the chaos. Pacts are made and then broken but by 1013 AD England's resistance collapses. Swain Forkbeard, a formidable man with a temper to match, is finally recognised as King of England but soon dies and his son Cnut is raised to the throne. Cnut provides much needed peace and strengthens his position by marriage to the defeated Saxon King's widow who is also, and conveniently, sister of the Duke of Normandy. Cnut's vision to rule a North Sea Empire including Norway and Denmark is short lived for, upon his death in 1035 AD, there follows troubled years which see the rise of several Saxon dynasties, the most noticeable being the family of Earl Godwine.

From obscure origins in Sussex the Godwine family rise to power in just two generations with the marriage of his daughter, Edith, to the new Saxon King, Edward the Confessor.

The old rivalries which re-emerge between Wales and Saxon England would pit two dominant leaders against each other. Harold, son of the Earl Godwine, inherits his father's estate, Wessex, then adds Hereford to his Earldom to become the power behind Edward the Confessor's throne. He thwarts the ambitions of a rebellious Mercia before turning his army on Wales where an ambitious and ruthless ruler, named Gruffydd, had removed all challenges to his authority. Lacking the qualities of a statesman his enemies in Wales are also numerous. He proves unable to resist Harold who organises a brilliant campaign by land and sea, driving Gruffydd from his stronghold at Rhuddlan into Mid Wales where fellow countrymen seize their chance for revenge. They turn on him and send Gruffydd's head to Saxon Harold.

Wales is once more broken up into separate kingdoms governed by different rulers and England no longer has to face a strong and dangerous neighbour west of Offa's Dyke.

Then, in January 1066 AD, Edward the Confessor dies and Harold takes the throne claiming this had been granted him upon Edward's death bed. Across the Channel however, William, Duke of Normandy, states that he had been promised the throne and threatens to invade. While in the north another threat to England's new ruler had arrived on the north east coast. The Vikings were back with a massive army that marched on York beating all resistance.

King Harold had waited all summer for the Normans on the south coast but he could not ignore the age old enemy. At the head of 6,000 men King Harold marches north and on the dawn of the 20th day of September attacks the Viking host. The battle rages until nightfall when the Norwegians are beaten and the survivors flee.

Then, during the celebration feast that followed, King Harold receives news which would change the course of English history and bring an end to Saxon rule.

The Normans had landed.

As descendants of Viking settlers, led by Rollo 170 years earlier, they had left Normandy with the largest invasion force since Roman times and led by William the Bastard, Duke of Normandy, land on the Sussex coast on the 28th day of September 1066 AD.

Norman Conquest had begun and though Wales had failed to fulfil the ancient prophecy a national spirit had evolved and a politically recognised nation formed. But this new, and even more deadly foe, would leave the Welsh not only defending their land but fighting for its very survival.

Norman Conquest

King Harold marches his weary army south, gathering reinforcements, then moves out to meet this new challenge hoping for another victory but the Duke of Normandy with his army of Norman followers and adventurers waited in all their armoured splendour at Hastings. The Saxon warriors, many oath sworn to victory or death, form the traditional shield walls. Then, on the morning of the fourteenth day of October 1066 AD the invaders attack and having brought two thousand horses use them to devastating effect, charging again and again into the Saxon wall. The shields hold until dusk but Harold falls, pierced by arrows and soon the field is lost and William the Conqueror is victorious. On Christmas day he is crowned, King of England.

In the following years William completes a systematic destruction of all resistance far into the north and ruthlessly crushes any challenge to his role.

King William of England, Duke of Normandy and Count of Maine, employs his feudal ideas brought from France and grants newly won lands to loyal followers creating Lordships and establishing a new class system. Three of these Lordships are appointed for the sole purpose of the conquest of Wales. Hugh of Avranches becomes Earl of Chester, Roger Montgomery becomes Earl of Shrewsbury and William Fitz Osbern becomes the Earl of Hereford. They possess the authority to act virtually independently and by the year 1070 AD advance across Offa's Dyke.

Amidst the leaderless confusion in Wales attention turns to the east and faced by the Norman threat hasty alliances begin to form but with the deaths of notable leaders political chaos escalates leaving the Normans a divided front of which they take full advantage.

The Earl of Chester empowers his deputy, Robert, to advance along the north coast while Montgomery secures his base by building castles at Oswestry and Montgomery before crossing Offa's Dyke. Fitz Osborn also consolidates his hold by building mote and bailey structures for his garrisons. The frontier is dangerous and Welsh resistance aggressive though disjointed due to dynastic feuds and internal divisions. To compensate, the Earls offer Norman settlers and knights extra social and economic advantages. This policy would eventually lead to the foundation of the Marches, a buffer zone of Lordships between the Celtic west and Norman England.

On the North Wales coast Robert moves on Conwy and Caernarfon where he begins a policy of stern repression. He slaughters without mercy and forces captives into harsh slavery.

The ruler of Gwynedd, Trahaearn, continues to fight Robert but his authority is about to be challenged by a young man, Gruffydd ap Cynan (Gruffydd son of Cynan), a descendant of Rhodri Mawr whose family had been living as exiles in Ireland since his grandfather's murder in 1039 AD. His father had married into a ruling Viking family and with their aid Gruffydd was returning to claim his birthright, the Kingdom of Gwynedd.

After many twists and turns and broken alliances Gruffydd ap Cynan's ambitions eventually win through but in this same year, 1081 AD, King William I dies and the throne passes to his son so incorporating another custom from Normandy of the first born's right of succession unlike the ancient Celtic method, 'gavel kind,' with equal division amongst sons.

King William II tricks Gruffydd into a peace conference at Corwen and takes him captive then continues against the turmoil in South and Mid Wales where a weakened Lord Rhys is forced into battle. In 1093 AD Rhys ap Teudwr, also a descendant of Rhodri Mawr, is killed fighting the Normans in Brecon.

This same year Gruffydd escapes to lead a daring raid with just three ships and kills the hated Robert at the foot of the Great Orme near Llandudno, but against the threat of a two pronged Norman attack can only return under the auspices of William II.

Upon William's death in 1100 AD the throne passes to his brother, Henry I. Gruffydd makes peace with the new King having learnt the hard way to keep the Norman armies out of Gwynedd. Wales as a whole though was not faring well with the Normans now holding all lands east of the River Conwy, most of central Powys, Pembrokeshire and Morgannwy. The Normans' fragile grip along the border is also tightened as important families establish themselves in the Marches where under protection of the Earls their Lordships begin to evolve into recognisable units.

King Henry's ambitions, however, are focused on the continent where he defeats the King of France and expands this Kingdom to its most powerful yet but his death in 1135 AD leaves a crisis, for his only son had predeceased him. By rights his daughter, Matilda, should succeed but many doubt the ability of a woman and civil war ensues. As a result the son of Adela, daughter of William the Conqueror, claims the throne but King Stephen can only provide weak and indecisive leadership.

The crisis in England provides a much needed reprieve for Wales but Gruffydd dies an old man and apart from his domain of Gwynedd hopes of independence are bleak indeed yet the threads were coming together as leaders begin to emerge who might be strong enough to hold off the Normans.

From the chaos two men emerge, one the son of Gruffydd named Owain Gwynedd and the other named after his grandfather, Lord Rhys. They expand their Welsh Kingdoms and together raise an army to challenge the divided Normans. However, a new King was about to rise to the English throne. Matilda's second marriage to Geoffrey Plantagenet, the heir of Anjou, had born a son they named Henry.

King Stephen had been beset by trouble throughout his realm as disinherited kinsmen revive baronial claims and the continental Kingdom splits away. By 1154 AD his effective rule only covers south east England and he is left no option but to surrender the succession to Geoffrey and Matilda's son, Henry Plantagenet.

Henry II, already Due of Normandy, Count of Anjou, and by marriage, Duke of Aquitaine, was now also King of England. Aged twenty one he had become the most powerful ruler in Europe with his cross channel Kingdom stretching from the Scottish borders to the Pyrenees. Henry soon shows he is master in his own house and despite the vast responsibilities of his Kingdom including bitter quarrels with the Archbishop of Canterbury, Thomas a Becket, turns his attention west to crush Welsh resistance.

Owain and Rhys join forces with Powys and men from all over Wales, seething discontent at Norman oppression, march to Corwen, on the banks of the River Dee, where they prepare to make their stand. Yet the Norman style of warfare with mounted knights was suited to open ground and before engaging the Welsh forces must first overcome the land itself.

In July 1165 AD the largest army ever assembled for the conquest of Wales gathers in readiness at Oswestry and Shrewsbury. Beneath their swirling banners the finest knights of

France, and the flower of the Norman army, lead the vast column up the Ceiriog Valley towards the uninviting slope of the Berwyn mountains, beyond which lies Corwen. It is the height of summer yet the rain is torrential and whipped by howling winds. For mile after mile the great army trudges through thick heather and bog, all the while assailed by the Welsh, until slowly the column grinds to a halt. Then, without even a glimpse of Owain and Rhys's army, is forced to turn back and wonder at the Welsh ability to turn the weather against them. King Henry is furious but can only vent his spleen on captives, twenty two of whom are mutilated to death including two of Owain's own sons, and ravage the Welsh borders. The King would return, but as a statesman, not a soldier.

Upon Owain's death, five years later, it is Gwynedd's turn for division as his offspring turn on each other. Two of his sons, Madog and Rhiryd, are so disgusted they leave Wales with eight ships, reputedly in search of a new land far to the west, sailing into legend and a life in the New World.

Three years after Owain's death a grandson of his is born, deep in Gwynedd's mountain vastness at Dodelwyddelan Castle, into the political rivalries now dominating the north. His name, Llywelyn ap Iorwerth, would one day ring throughout the land when he continues the great deeds of the Lord Rhys whose status had finally been recognised by King Henry.

The Lord Rhys, now secure in his Kingdom, Deheubarth, turns his energies to good government, poetry and the arts. The first Eisteddfod (competitions between poets or Bards) is held and the words of an ancient prophecy remembered after decades of violent struggle to survive. These Bards would play a crucial role in the future development of Wales speaking encouraging, enticing and passionate words against the swords of England.

In 1189 AD, upon Henry II's death, Richard I succeeds as the new King and uses his resources to recover lost domains in France. To this end Richard spends just seven months of his ten year rule on brief visits to England and leads crusades to the Holy Land until his death in 1199 AD when the different parts of the empire chose different heirs and the Barons of England and Normandy opt for his younger brother, John.

A great contest between an English King and a Welsh Prince was developing, for Wales also had undergone many changes.

After the death of Lord Rhys, in 1197 AD, his Kingdom, Deubeubarth, saw itself torn apart by his unruly sons but in the north the grandson of Owain, Llywelyn ap Iorwerth, had risen to rule many of his kinsmen and walking in the footsteps of Rhys he too would prove himself a patron of the arts and a leader of the Welsh to be reckoned with. He becomes the dominant force in Gwynedd, makes an ally with Powys and stabilises south Wales by dividing Deheubarth and Ceredigion amongst descendants of Lord Rhys.

All along the border the Marcher Lords grow discontent with the new King's interfering policies so begin to flex their independent muscles. To counter this threat King John lays aside his differences with the Welsh and cleverly concludes a treaty with Llywelyn who proves true to his word with John and protects the King's interests along the turbulent border.

As a reward for Llywelyn's loyalty, King John arranges the marriage of his youngest and much loved, though illegitimate, daughter to the Welsh leader. Llywelyn accepts the marriage and retires with his new wife, Joan, to his royal Maenol near Aber on the North Wales coast, located between the mountains and the sea.

Meanwhile, King John's problems were mounting. He returns from wars in Ireland to an England which now lies under a papal interdict. John, ever stubborn, refuses to accept Pope Innocent III's nominee, Stephen Langton, as Archbishop of Canterbury so finds himself excommunicated and his English Lords released from their oaths of fealty by the Pope.

Contemplating the possibility of an alliance between these rebellious Marcher Lords and Wales, King John makes yet another serious error of judgement and attacks Llywelyn. Realising he cannot defeat the King in outright battle, Llywelyn can only seek refuge, as many of his ancestors had done, in Snowdonia's wild mountains. From this retreat he arranges a meeting between Joan and her father but is made to accept a shameful treaty confining him to his original estates.

Llywelyn though is not a man to submit easily and with their fierce pride humiliated by King John the Welsh people turn to Llywelyn as the leader who could throw off English domination.

Already facing the restless Barons under his tyrannical rule, King John had now lost a powerful ally and with the Pope urging the King of France to invade and depose him, John was in dire need of friends. Faced by civil war, invasion and a full blown Welsh revolt, King John can only submit to the Pope.

Taking full advantage of England's turmoil, Llywelyn persuades all the Welsh Princes, including his old adversary, Gwynwynwyn, to join in a patriotic alliance. By 1214 AD

Llywelyn forces John into a truce and regains all his previous power and takes the title, 'Prince of Aberffraw,' where so long ago his distant ancestors had begun to build a Kingdom, and 'Lord of Snowdon.' A mountainous land in the heart of Gwynedd where so many invaders had failed to beat Welsh resistance.

In England the rebel Barons had no clear leader to replace King John so devise a new kind of revolt and introduce a programme of reform by which all would swear to abide.

They call this reform, the Magna Carta, the Great Charter.

Llywelyn wins many clauses in the Magna Carta granting the Welsh significant concession. All lands lost to the Welsh are returned and Welsh law, as opposed to the Marcher or English laws, would apply. He also wins the return of hostages including his son by his first marriage, Gruffydd.

True to form, however, King John takes little notice of the Charter and as a peace treaty it fails, yet the rights of a subject against the crown had been recognised. England had entered an era when such methods would become standard procedure for opposition but for now the civil wars go on.

Llywelyn continues to side against John and supports the de Braose family in regaining their Marcher realm little knowing how these two families would become tragically intertwined. He also demonstrates his statesmanship in Wales after the death of the Prince of Deheubarth by calling an assembly where various claimants gain land. Llywelyn presides over the meeting but refuses to hold any territories himself and governs along the lines of the Magna Carta.

Then, in October 1216 AD, King John dies but his heir, Henry III, is only a minor and so the Kingdom is governed by a council of state, led by the Regent of England. This Regent, William Marshall, had risen from being a landless esquire, won a kingly reputation in the tournaments and was now maintaining fidelity to his fourth Plantagenet King. His regime also recognises Llywelyn's status but still keeps a tight grip of the south Wales' coast and Pembrokeshire.

To maintain the unity Llywelyn had striven so hard for, a solemn council is held in 1221 AD at Shrewsbury where Dafydd, his son by Joan, is recognised as his sole heir by the young King Henry III, the Justicar, a Papal legate and the Archbishop of Canterbury. Then, a marriage is arranged, one of many in a complex web throughout the Marches, between his daughter, Helen, and the son of the powerful Earl of Chester, securing his northern border.

A friendship develops between the new King and Llywelyn, who agrees to protect Henry's interests along the Marches, so when William de Braose rebels against the crown Llywelyn attacks his Marcher Lordship and takes William prisoner.

Given the freedom of Llywelyn's manor the captivity is anything but arduous until the Welsh Prince returns from a hunting trip to discover his beloved Joan and the much younger de Braose indulging their affair. In his fury, Llywelyn hangs de Braose, imprisons his wife, then turns his rage on England forcing Henry to send troops to quell the constant attacks, damaging the mighty efforts to build a politically recognised Wales.

Llywelyn realises this and restores Joan to her place of honour, then makes peace with Henry.

Llywelyn is now the undisputed ruler and Wales can turn away from warfare to a period of enlightenment. Scholarly and artistic achievements increase, Celtic traditions and literature are encouraged while mighty stone castles and abbeys are built.

Welsh law is also enforced, laws, the principal of which, originated with Hywel Dda during the 10th century.

Then, upon Joan's death, and as a mark of his deep respect, a new burial place is founded on Ynys Mon where Franciscan Friars would pray constantly for the repose of her soul.

By the age of sixty seven Llywelyn retreats to Aberconwy Abbey where, in 1240 AD, he dies, humbly wearing the traditional habit of a lay brother. This self styled custodian of the Welsh Kingdoms had never called himself, 'Prince of Wales,' but as recognition for his supreme efforts he is awarded a title only one other man had proved worthy of. The people name him Llywelyn Fawr, 'The Great.'

As arranged his son, Dafydd, takes his place but one of Dafydd's first acts is to imprison his half brother, Gruffydd, plus two of Gruffydd's sons, but many are discontent by such a move and pay King Henry to intervene. The King forces Dafydd to hand the three captives over to him but instead of releasing them sends them to the Tower of London. For three years they remain locked up before making good their escape. Whilst climbing from the window the sheet rope breaks and Gruffydd falls to his death. Dafydd's rule, however, proves short lived with his death in 1246 AD and the carefully laid plans of his father to maintain a united Wales start to crumble. Another dark era was fast approaching when the Welsh face an English King who proves their most formidable opponent yet. Their greatest enemy though would be internal division.

Gruffydd's two sons who escaped from the Tower, Owain and Dafydd, return to North Wales and straight into conflict with their brother, named after his illustrious grandfather, Llywelyn, who had begun to seize control in the north. Their armies meet at Bryn Derwin, where gentle hills merge with the harsh peaks of Snowdonia. Llywelyn is victorious and casts his brothers in prison and in 1258 AD assumes the title, Prince of Wales.

Over the next twelve years Llywelyn clears the English armies from his eastern borders and comes into conflict for the first time with the future King, the Lord Edward, who was proving a highly capable leader.

Discontent with the King's rule, led by the forceful Earl of Leicester, Simon de Montfort, had resulted in civil war all along the Marches and it would be the Lord Edward's military campaign that culminates in Simon's death at the Battle of Evesham. This future King was honing his special talent for war, and in so doing, restored his father's full power.

With Llywelyn now Governor of the three main provinces of Wales, Gwynedd, Powys and Deheubarth, King Henry is compelled to accept his status and peace is restored with the Treaty of Montgomery. Llywelyn is the first Welsh leader to be recognised as Prince of Wales by an English King. Following in his grandfather's footsteps he holds court at Aberffraw on Ynys Mon, in the ancient palace still adorned with stone heads carved by his forbears.

In 1272 AD Henry III dies and his son rises to the throne. This new King, Edward I, would prove himself the most war like and ruthless, yet for now is content to encourage the divisions amongst the Welsh while he puts down the simmering revolt of the Barons. Llywelyn recognises the new King but expects the same in return, as equals. Edward though had other ideas.

Llywelyn had released one of his brothers but Dafydd's affections still lay with Owain who would remain a prisoner in Dolbardon Castle for twenty years. Dafydd and Gruffydd ap Gwynwynwyn, ruler of southern Powys, both plot to assassinate the Prince but fail and flee to England where they are well received by Edward.

With the King's support Dafydd begins a series of raids into Wales but Edward's next move was about to, as no doubt intended, infuriate Llywelyn.

Llywelyn's future bride, Eleanor, daughter of Simon de Montefort, now dwelt in exile. He arranges her return so they may marry but en-route she is waylaid in the English Channel and imprisoned by Edward. Then, in 1277 AD, Edward I sets a major offensive against the Welsh Prince in motion which is designed to take Llywelyn's land a piece at a time, driving him back into Gwynedd where he can be finished off. Dafydd, backed by Edward's soldiery, leads one of the three pronged attacks from the royal castles of Chester, Montgomery and Caernarfon.

Llywelyn cannot hold back the joint Welsh and English advance and is soon trapped west of the Conwy River. He can only strike a deal, but the price is high. He is allowed to keep his title yet forfeit the allegiance of all Welsh Princes and is left only the heartland of Gwynedd. Then, in the company of those who supported him, he travels to London where he must perform homage to the King. Upon receiving Llywelyn's acceptance of his supremacy, King Edward agrees to the marriage with Eleanor but takes complete control of the wedding.

So humiliating is the experience they resolve to die in their native land rather than yield again.

Then, King Edward continues the humiliation by sending many officials into Wales to run local governments. Oppression by these Royal bailiffs soon bites deep and slowly support begins to return to Llywelyn.

Throughout the north gatherings take place and the inspiring oratory of Llywelyn stokes the people's disaffection towards the tyranny of English rule. Talk turns to planning as the Welsh nobles, except for Gwynwynwyn and Rhys ap Maredudd, join the cause. They create a fine company representing all the major ruling houses but a spark would prematurely ignite the tinder.

Dafydd lived in lands granted by the King but he felt bitter having suffered broken promises, ridicule and constant harassment from royal officials. Finally, his loyalties turn again and on 21st March 1282 he attacks the English border castle at Hawarden, kills the garrison and captures its Lord, Roger de Clifford. Dafydd had returned to his roots.

Suddenly the rising explodes from the mountain fortress of Snowdonia and Meirionnydd. Swift attacks are unleashed in mid Wales and along the borders. A large force led by Welsh nobles attack Oswestry, southern Lords capture castles and in Ceredigion the Royal castle at Aberystwyth is taken.

Throughout the land similar deeds are accomplished but the odds against Wales begin to grow to terrible proportions for in response King Edward I planned a crushing retaliation.

Edward begins to gather the strength of his realm. Men are called to arms, sheriffs organise provisions, extra horses are shipped from France and orders to recruit more cavalry and crossbow men are sent to all his domains. A fleet of fifty ships begins to assemble off the coast of Ynys Mon (Anglesey), the bread basket of North Wales, and noblemen of the first rank are placed in charge of their commands. The Earl of Gloucester commands in the south west, the Earl of Hereford Constable of England, takes command in Brecon while Roger Mortimer, one of the most powerful Marcher Lords, takes charge of Montgomery.

King Edward I places himself at the head of his main army at Flint. Then, on 8th April 1282 AD these huge armies begin to move and the fight for Wales begins.

The Welsh resist fiercely but of Llywelyn himself little is heard. Now, nearly sixty years old he stays close to his wife, Eleanor, for she is expecting their first born and the Welsh Prince waited for his heir. In June a girl child is born, not the male heir he prayed for. His beloved wife dies giving birth to Gwenllion and Llywelyn can only turn aside from his tragedy to ride south with a troop of armed men, venting his sorrow in battle and sending tremors throughout the Marches.

Everywhere the Welsh were being pushed back, particularly in the north with Luke de Tany's invasion fleet taking Ynys Mon (Anglesey) and Edward's army reaching the River Conwy.

Llywelyn speeds north to aide his brother in the defence of their mountain stronghold from where they can only sally forth on raids and wait for the onset of winter. At the daunting thought of a winter campaign Edward offers negotiations but then the King declares himself and his devious plan unfolds, the trap sprung.

From the hills overlooking Ynys Mon the Prince's men spy the English army move and they pour down to do battle. Though victorious this could only be the beginning of the end, unless the south would rise once more in support. Dafydd stays to defend the north while Llywelyn rides south to call upon their loyalties. He enters southern Powys in December and after resting a Cwm Hir Abbey moves his army into the hilly lands around Builth. Then, confident his army can hold, he slips away on a mysterious errand.

An English army, commanded by Roger le Strange, approached from the east and where the rivers Wye and Irfon meet he finds the bridge defended by Llywelyn's men. With the two armies deadlocked a surprise attack is mounted on the river crossing.

With no clear battlefield many become separated from the fighting and one such contingent, led by Stephen Frankton, come upon what he believes to be a minor Welsh Chief supported by his servants. The English knights give chase along the misty valley and Frankton runs the Chief through with his lance then duty done rides away in search of the battle unaware of the man's true identity. By chance servants of Edmund Mortimer find Llywelyn ap Gruffydd, Prince of Wales and Lord of Snowdon, where he lay, mortally wounded by a lance thrust. With his dying breath he asks for a priest but none came.

On the battlefield, unaware of the Princes demise, the fighting goes on and soon many noble names lie amongst the dead.

Then, in his camp on Wales' north coast, King Edward receives a report from Roger le Strange, "know sire that the forces that you placed under my command fought Llywelyn ap Gruffydd in the land of Builth on Friday, after the feast of St. Nicholas, and that Llywelyn ap Gruffydd is dead, his army broken and all the flower of his men killed, as the bearer of this letter will tell you."

Along with the report Edward is handed proof of the victory, Llywelyn's head.

Prince Llywelyn's headless body is carried to Cwm Hir Abbey and given a decent burial but his head is sent by King Edward to be displayed at the Tower of London where it is crowned with a circlet of ivy in derision of the Welsh seers who for centuries had told of a Celtic King who would one day regain the Crown.

The sense of loss spreads throughout Wales and many in Gwynedd who supported Llywelyn refuse to fight for the renegade, Dafydd. As the circle tightens in the new year he retreats to Dolbardarn Castle in the Llanberis Pass then, on 28th June 1283 AD, Dafydd is captured by Welshmen in the service of the King. His wife and children are imprisoned along with Llywelyn's baby girl, Gwenllion, who would be raised in a nunnery, never to even know of her father or his noble deeds.

Dafydd is taken to Shrewsbury where he is condemned and dragged through the streets by horses to the High Cross. Here he is partially hanged then his entrails are ripped out and the body chopped into quarters. These are sent to Bristol, York, Northampton and Winchester but his head is displayed on The Tower of London, next to his brother's.

With the last native born Prince of Wales now dead, King Edward's policies would also take the last vestige of Wales' independence and with no option must now accept English rule.

In 1284 the King draws up the Statute of Rhuddlan to arrange the future government of Wales. Then, to enforce his rule, employs Master Giles of St. George at great expense to build mighty stone castles.

The King's son, also named Edward, is then given the title, 'Prince of Wales,' as the first, in what would become a long tradition, for the English King's heir.

The Rise of Owain Glyndŵr

Wales had been conquered yet the ancient prophecy still told of a leader who would regain Welsh independence and go on to win the crown of England, but even to challenge English domination would take a very special leader, one possessing the qualities of all the great names from the past.

Now that the house of Gwynedd had come to an end the emphasis would eventually shift to Powys, once a great Kingdom reaching from the Dee estuary in the north east and far into mid Wales. In 1236 AD the King of Powys died and the Kingdom became divided between the north and south by the River Dee. Gruffydd Maelor II ruled in the north and married Emma, daughter of Lord Audley, who bore him four sons. Of these sons the eldest, named Madog, inherited Castell Dinas Bran, overlooking Llangollen, while his brother, Gruffydd, received the Manor of Glyndyfrdwy, meaning, 'valley of the waters of the Dee,' further along the beautiful vale.

In the wars that followed Madog was killed while Gruffydd continued to fight alongside Prince Llywelyn to the bitter end. Then, as the ancient Kingdoms of Wales were dissolved and reshaped the victorious King Edward I granted lands to those he pardoned. Once such, Gruffydd, received a portion of his manor at Glyndyfrdwy. A mark of the King's generosity and powerful statement that he now ruled. Dinas Bran, however, became part of the Marcher Kingdom, Chirkland.

From this small manor nestling the winding river the family estate grows within two generations to include Cynllaith near the Shropshire border where the chief house is built at Sycharth, 'a fair wooden house standing upon four wondrous pillars on the crest of a green hill.' The wealthy owner, named , like his grandfather, Gruffydd Fychan, had won many riches fighting on the Continent alongside the Black Prince. He marries Helen Goch, the daughter of the Lord of Tregarn, a descendent of the House of Deheubarth, who owned lands in south Cardiganshire and north Pembrokeshire merging two powerful Welsh families and the result would be a boy child, a son of Powys and a descendant of ancient lines.

In 1327 the weak and inept leadership of Edward II had resulted in the revolt, led partly by Roger Mortimer, which deposed the King. With a new ruler on the throne the Crown's interests in France were reawakened and began what would become known as the Hundred Years War.

At the battle of Crechy, in 1346, Edward III's army won an overwhelming victory over King Philip VI, while back in England his northern army routs the invading Scots. Flushed with success the King and his son, the Black Prince, create a stable regime but they would soon find themselves short of the funds to continue their campaigns in France.

Increased taxes brought yet more hardship to people who had already faced harsh winters and poor crop yields. In Europe an economic slump created a devalued currency and low prices for produce. The people became poorer, yet still the taxes rose as famine began to gnaw their stomachs.

In Wales particularly the people felt themselves a colony ruled solely for the King's profit.

Then, with terrible swiftness, the Black Death spread across Europe and many began to speak of the 'End of the World.' One in every three dies but in the wake of such a death toll new lives are also beginning.

One such newborn is the son of Helen Goch and Gruffydd, who misses the birth while fighting beside the Black Prince in France. Helen's ancestry stretched back to Prince Llywelyn's daughter and so the bloodlines of three ancient houses of Powys, Deheubarth and Gwynedd, were fused into this boy. They name him, Owain, and in the family's main home at Sycharth his childhood passes listening to the Bards and their tales of ancient prophecies, while all around him life grew steadily harder.

Discontent amongst the Welsh people is ignored except by John of Gaunt, Duke of Lancaster. He calls for the repair and restocking of neglected castles to maintain the suppression but the ageing King is focused only on his need to raise the money needed to counter his losses in France. The Poll Tax is introduced in 1369. A year later Owain's father dies, never to know the heights to which his son would rise and Owain inherits the family estates.

In keeping with tradition, at the age of twelve, Owain becomes a Page to the Earl of Arundel at Chirk Castle where he can learn the rules of chivalry and courtly behaviour. He receives a good education, speaking Latin, French and English as well as his native Welsh.

Meanwhile, with the death of his eldest son, the now senile King chooses his grandson to succeed him and in 1377 the ten year old boy becomes King Richard II.

As the new King settled upon his throne, Owain travels to London and enrols at the Inns of Court where he can study law. Whilst here the young man meets his future wife, Margaret, daughter of Sir David Hanmer, a Justice of the King's Bench. The knowledge he gains of law and government would prove of great value and strongly influence his future actions, as would his next endeavours.

After his marriage Owain enters military service in 1384 as a Squire to Sir Degory Sais, a Welsh Captain in command at Berwick upon Tweed on the Scottish border. He takes his military training seriously and gains his first experience of war against the Scots. Owain's bravery is noticed by the King and he is chosen to become Richard's shield bearer in the continuing campaigns in France. Above all else, Owain proves himself a soldier.

In 1387 Owain returns from fighting to Chirk Castle where he serves as a retainer, at the age of twenty eight. Then, two years later, acts as Esquire to a man who is destined to become his mortal enemy, a man powerful enough to seize the throne, the bold and ambitious, Henry Bolingbroke.

King Richard II had turned into a self willed monarch causing political tension amongst the Barons to spill over but the King had secured a truce with France by marrying the seven year old Isabella of Valois in 1396 and this allowed him to concentrate on England.

While his new bride lived alone in Winchester Castle the King ruthlessly uses his personal power to crush the Barons resistance and orders the execution of the Earl of Arundel, Owain's mentor for so long, while the Earl of Gloucester is murdered and the Earls of Warwick, Mowbray and eventually Henry Bolingbroke, find themselves exiled. Henry was the eldest surviving son of the Duke of Lancaster, John of Gaunt, who, as one of the King's uncles, had virtually ruled England throughout Richard's youth. Henry had grown alongside him and won a reputation for courage. He now bore the titles, Earl of Derby, Duke of

Hereford, and upon his father's death, inherited the Dukedom of Lancaster, but as one of King Richard's most active opponents, looses possession of his lands and is banished from the realm for ten years.

Meanwhile, Owain had retired to his family's chief house at Sycharth with its great chimney where blazing fires greet the numerous guests and settles with his wife to raise their six sons and five daughters.

Owain manages his estates fairly but enjoys nothing more than the regular hunting trips to his lodge in a valley so beautiful the Pagans believed it blessed by the Gods and the river's surging waters to be magical. Here, in the Vale of Llangollen, he would stay in the family's Manor of Glyndyfrdwy, meaning, 'valley of the waters,' and become so taken with the place, take its name for his own.

Owain Glyndŵr could see, however, the ever increasing taxes, the galling exclusion of Welshmen from high office and the commercial privileges enjoyed by the English settlers who dwelt around their strongholds like islands in a Welsh sea. A century was passing since such resentment had exploded into full blown war, a hundred years of change leading to the same inevitable conclusion and Owain would find himself the heart and hope of Wales.

Then, a dispute arises with his neighbour, the fierce Marcher Lord, Reginald de Grey of Ruthin, who decides to increase his lands by taking territories that lie under Owain's domain but, using his legal skills, Owain takes the matter to London and wins King Richard's support of his claim.

However, with events in England moving so quickly and the

changes that were about to unfold, this dispute had only just begun.

In 1399, and thinking his realm now secure, King Richard sails with his army to extinguish the rebellion of the Irish Chief, MacMurrogh. The expedition was going badly when in July the King receives news that his cousin, Henry Bolingbroke, had returned to claim his lands and reform the government.

With the six year old heir apparent, Edmund Mortimer, still alive he would not openly seek the throne, but support for Henry was growing rapidly as many nobles join his standard. Among them, Percy, the mighty Earl of Northumberland, his son, Hotspur and Ralph Neville, Earl of Westmorland. Upon hearing of this growing army marching south, King Richard travels to Chester but finds support dwindling. Then, as Henry's entourage approaches, he flees to Conwy where he receives the treacherous news that the Royal army had been disbanded. Richard wanders North Wales confused when he is tricked and made captive, then, on 21st September, enters the Tower of London a prisoner and the last of the Plantagenet Kings.

Nine days later Richard signs a formal renunciation of the Crown and in reply Henry claims, by descent from Henry II, the right to govern the realm. King Henry IV is crowned, but with this rise of the House of Lancaster, repercussions would be felt throughout the Kingdom for many years to come.

After his abdication, Richard is moved to Pontefract Castle in Yorkshire where he dies in mysterious circumstances at the age of thirty three.

The new King honours his young son, also named Henry, with the titles, Earl of Chester and Prince of Wales, while many of his close friends and supporters are also granted high positions. One of these men is the Lord of Ruthin, Reginald de Grey, who is promoted to the King's council.

Reginald de Grey's forebears had held the Lordship of Ruthin since Edward I's conquest in 1282, but with a desire to expand his lands, de Grey was about to ignite an even more devastating war.

Many notable names, both Welsh and English, were destined for great deeds, without doubt the most obscure would be the rise of the name, Tudwr.

As descendents of Ednyfed Fychan, who had been Seneschal (Chief Administrator) and confidante to Llywelyn Fawr, 'The Great,' they came from a notable Welsh lineage. Particularly as Ednyfed's wife, Gwenllian, was daughter of Prince Rhys of South Wales. Ednyfed's grandson, Tudwr ap Gronowy, was in effect founder of the Tudwr line and as a great patron of the Bards he owned extensive lands along the North Wales coast, Ynys Môn and Caernarfonshire.

His grandson, Goronwy ap Tudwr II, maintained close links with Owain Glyndŵr which were further strengthened by his marriage to Owain's sister. Their four sons, Gwyilym, Goronwy, Rhys and Maredudd, would also prove close supporters of Owain in the coming conflict and play a pivotal role but Maredudd's son, named after Owain, would unwittingly set incredible events in motion.

However, all this was yet to pass and Wales is rocked by even higher taxes levied by the King, Henry IV. Like his fellow Welshmen, Owain is furious then, for the second time his neighbour, Reginald de Grey, descends upon Owain's lands.

Again, Owain seeks justice in London but the new King decides in favour of his friend, Lord de Grey, and orders Owain to grant further concessions.

The Bishop of St. Asaph, John Trevor, fails to mediate with the contemptuous council and can only warn them that the consequences of such actions could prove dire. However, their insults continue to ring in Owain's ears and he returns to Sycharth bitter at this new injustice.

King Henry IV then sets off to invade Scotland and calls for English and Welsh nobles to follow him to war. Reginald de Grey is given the task of delivering the message to Owain, which arrives too late for him to mobilise his troops. The campaign in the north goes badly for the King and he authorises Lord de Grey to seize Owain's whole estate under the pretext of forfeiture for high treason.

Unaware of any treachery, Owain receives an invitation to reconcile with de Grey who visits his home in Sycharth. Then, as English troops surround the house, Owain's Bard, Iolo Goch, plays a harp song in Welsh, warning him of the deceit. Owain escapes but is now a fugitive in his own land and left with only one choice.

On the sixteenth day of September, in the year 1400, Owain Glyndŵr, accompanied by his brother and eldest son, attend a secret meeting with a number of leading Welsh figures outside the tiny hamlet now known as Llidiart y Parc, (Gateway to the Park), in the Manor of Glyndyfrdwy, once Owain's prized hunting park and now confiscated by the Crown. This beautiful valley, threaded by the River Dee, was about to witness history in the making. They proclaim Owain, 'Prince of Wales,' a symbolic statement to both the people of Wales and England, that this would be a war for independence.

Two weeks later, as Lord de Grey's township of Ruthin prepared to host a Fair celebrating St. Mathew's Day, Owain leads two hundred and fifty men, disguised as peasants, into the fortified town. After unleashing their pent up anger only three buildings, including the Castle, are left untouched. Then, in rapid succession they sack the English townships of Denbigh, Rhuddlan, Flint and Hawarden before moving south to Oswestry and Welshpool where they finally meet stiff resistance, led by the Sheriff of Shropshire, and the small Welsh force can only scatter.

Upon hearing of the rebellion, King Henry comes from the north and marches his army through Wales where he proceeds to burn and plunder in a path of devastation until he reaches Ynys Mon, 'Anglesey,' where he is attacked by angry Welshmen, led by the Tudwrs. King Henry is forced to seek refuge in Beaumaris Castle until his army can regain control but before he returns to England, Henry sacks the Franciscan Monestary at Llanfaes, built by Llywelyn the Great, over the tomb of his wife Joan while the friars are turned out to starve.

Then, as the King's army begins the long march back they are assailed by the foulest weather causing horses to flounder, lost baggage and among the sick troops talk spreads of Owain's magical powers with which he can control the elements.

On reaching the safety of Shrewsbury, King Henry declares Owain Glyndŵr an outlaw and to make an example has the captured Gronwy ap (son of) Tudwr hung, drawn and quartered, then displays the pieces of his body along the border. In the new year, orders are sent to hunt Owain down.

Back on Ynys Mon, the remaining Tudwr brothers plan a daring raid on the impregnable Conwy Castle. They wait until Good Friday, when the garrison is at church outside its walls, then cut the guards throats and, with just forty men, capture the castle. The outcome, as intended, is a severe blow to English pride.

In reply, Henry appoints Hotspur, son of the powerful Earl of Northumberland, to command in Wales. He lays siege to the castle accompanied by the King's son, Prince Henry, on his first active duty in Wales.

The Tudwr's hold out for three months but in the end can only accept severe terms of surrender and must hand over nine men for execution.

After this successful outcome however, Hotspur is very discontent due to the lack of funds for his troops and returns to Northumberland from where the Percy family exert pressure on the King for recompense, but Henry has many expenses, including the defence of lands in France, protecting shipping and the Scottish borders. The money is not forthcoming and the rift between these two powerful families widens.

Throughout the Tudwr's daring campaign, Owain had been tireless, planning his actions and calling for support. One such letter is intercepted and the King, now expecting Owain to attack South Wales, summons the troops of fourteen shires, but the seasoned Owain, a veteran of many campaigns, knew the suicidal nature of facing such an army head on.

Reports of Owain's raids begin to place him all over and unable to check the daring Welsh guerrilla tactics, the King resorts to a 'Chevauchee,' burning all in his path. He makes no contact with Owain's forces so devastates the Monastery, Strata Florida, and executes those who choose death rather than betray Owain.

Then in a remote mountain glen in the high lands of Pumlomon, Owain faces his first major confrontation with a force comprising of 1,500 English soldiery and Flemish mercenaries marching north on the King's orders to destroy the revolt.

There could be only one outcome or Owain was finished.

With reputedly just one hundred and twenty men, mounted upon their tough hill ponies and armed with deadly longbows plus homemade weaponry, Owain engaged his enemy. Many are slaughtered with no quarter given before the battle of Mynydd Hyddgen is won.

News of victory against such overwhelming odds spreads like fire, enhancing Owain's reputation and causing Wales to erupt. More men are drawn to his leadership and soon he controls a great host that raid into Hereford and Shrewsbury where they cause much destruction, returning with flocks and herds to finance the war.

Welshpool and Montgomery are also devastated while the Royal castles of Aberystwyth, Harlech and Caernarfon, find themselves placed under siege, looking out upon Owain's standard, 'a golden dragon on a white field.'

Towards the year's end, uncertain how to proceed and lacking finance, King Henry states his wish to draw Owain back into Royal obedience. The Percy's of Northumberland agree and suggest that the return of Owain's lands are a small price to pay. Reginald de Grey, however, and John Beaufort, Earl of Hereford, who both hold Owain's confiscated lands, push for a military solution. The rebellion, they demand, must be crushed.

Owain realises he must seek active support from foreign allies to prevent English might massing against him. The Welsh cause gains support from the Irish Princes and King Henry is forced to send his son, Thomas, to oppress them while the combination of French and Scottish favour towards the Welsh proves very dangerous for the King, but commissions had already been sent to array troops in three key places.

In the new year of 1402, Owain and his men had plans of their own. They return to Ruthin, knowing de Grey to be in residence, and attack. The Lord of Ruthin sallies forth, seeing his chance to defeat Owain, but he is outwitted, his men killed and de Grey is taken captive.

Then, in the spring, a comet appears in the sky (now known as Hailey's comet) and the Welsh Bards take it on as an omen. As they sing of victory and ancient prophecies, Owain goes from strength to strength and while the English armies mass for their invasion, he engages his most daring plan yet and attacks Mortimer lands in Glamorgan and Gwent. The Mortimer's are a powerful Marcher family indeed and with young Edmund Mortimer's nephew, the heir apparent, still held by King Henry, are reluctant royal supporters and respond to the attack with two thousand heavily armed militia. Owain draws them into a killing ground at Bryn Glas leaving eight hundred English dead and takes captive the twenty six year old Edmund Mortimer.

By August the King's triple assault on Wales is ready to proceed, but the weather throws rain, then hail, and even snow, causing the advance to flounder. The King is nearly killed by a huge tent pole as it collapses in the storm while his men, forced to sleep in their rusting armour to stave off the cold, whisper about the wizard Owain who could send such forces of nature against them.

Owain Glyndŵr's reputation soared like the shooting star, visible for all to see. 'Surely,' the Bards sang, 'this is the leader the ancient prophets had foretold,' and no doubt Owain encouraged his Bards to intimidate the enemy while raising the hopes of a Nation long oppressed.

Certainly the impossible task of regaining Wales was now no longer a dream, but a belief.

Over the next two years the Welsh form their own council and parliament based at Machynlleth, while alliances with Scotland, France and the Pope, strengthen the claim of an independent Wales. The land, however, had suffered terrible destruction and to help raise money to rebuild the towns and abbeys Owain ransoms his arch enemy, Reginald de Grey. In so doing he maintains an honourable tradition yet demands a staggering ten thousand marks which would leave de Grey financially ruined for life.

King Henry assists with de Grey's ransom but refuses to help Edmund Mortimer. The Percy family are infuriated for they had helped Henry to the throne, held the Scottish borders and contained the revolt in Wales, at great cost. With no reimbursement and the abandonment of Edmund, they felt ungenerously treated. So incensed is Percy's son, Hotspur, that, as his name implies, he acts precipitately and marches south declaring open rebellion. For once Henry responds decisively and their armies clash at Shrewsbury where, in July 1403, he defeats and kills Hostpur.

The Percy's begin to feel more in common with the Welsh Prince, as does the captive Edmund.

By the year 1405 control of virtually all Wales lay in Welsh hands. The newly captured Harlech Castle becomes Owain's Head

Quarters and his Parliament produces his own chancery and seals while two universities are sited, one in the north and one in the south, to educate those needed to administer a country.

The long and bloody struggle, against all odds, had nearly been won.

Meanwhile, the Marcher Lord, Edmund Mortimer, held hostage by Owain and whose claim to the English throne rivalled the King's, moves over to the Welsh cause and marries Owain's daughter, Catherine. This alliance, plus support from the powerful Percy's of Northumberland, creates an audacious and ambitious plan.

This pact is sealed with the signing of the Tripartite Indenture, which gives Owain Wales and a large tract of western England, the Percy's the whole of the north and Mortimer the south east of England.

If they could defeat King Henry.

However, in this same year, English dominance begins to reassert itself. The political situation in Scotland no longer posed a threat and, with Ireland now suppressed, Wales would soon stand alone.

In March, the sixteen year old Prince Henry, who had been appointed Lieutenant in Wales and the Marches, by the King, was encamped in Grosmont Castle with his specially trained and mobile troops. Unaware of this force inside, the Welsh attack with eight thousand men when suddenly the gates are opened and Prince Henry's light cavalry pour out, scattering the Welsh army, capturing its leader plus Owain's brother in law, and kill many.

Only four days after this defeat, the Welsh survivors regroup to attack Usk, under the leadership of Owain's eldest son, Gruffydd. A fierce battle ensues on a hill called, Mynydd Pwll Melyn (hill of the yellow pool),but the day does badly. They fight desperately to the last and fifteen hundred of Owain's men are killed including his brother, Tudwr. Three hundred are taken captive, among them his son, Gruffydd. All are beheaded and their bodies thrown into the pool.

Such losses to the Welsh are crippling. Then, in June another disaster strikes as the Deputy Lieutenant of Ireland attacks Ynys Mon, 'Anglesey,' and ravages this island granary.

The tide was beginning to turn against Wales for as Prince Henry continued to gain victories along the border his father had marched north to put down the rebellious Percy's of Northumberland who can only flee into Scotland.

With support fading Owain makes a daring arrangement with his one remaining, though dwindling French ally, the Duke of Orleans, who sends a fighting force to help him. This French force is met by Owain with ten thousand Welshmen and they march on England, expecting and hoping to be joined by the many discontented Marcher Lords. Once over the border however, there is no such support. King Henry had done his job well in quelling the rebel Barons and now ordered the Sheriffs of eighteen shires to raise their men to arms and deal with this new threat.

The armies meet near Worcester and make camp each side of the valley. Both are evenly matched and unable to gain any advantage. Skirmishes and jousting between knights take place but the battle fails to commence. After eight days of this stalemate King Henry leaves the field knowing his enemy will simply starve with no support in England.

The Franco-Welsh army had come to nothing and could only return to Wales leaving the King a bloodless victory.

In the following two years Owain's hold begins to crumble as all south west Wales yields to England and with civil unrest in France he looses the last of his allies, causing Wales' foreign policies to collapse. With the land devastated and lacking food the Welsh struggle continues but by 1408, as the harshest winter in memory freezes the ground, Welsh fortunes were about to take an even darker turn.

By February the last of Owain's English allies, the Earl of Northumberland and Lord Bardolf, are killed at Bramham Moor while the young Prince Henry, now highly thought of for his recent triumphs, places Aberystwyth Castle under siege. By September it had fallen.

Meanwhile, Gilbert of Goodrich and Lord Furnival begin the siege of Harlech, Owain's headquarters, and to English delight he is trapped inside with the remaining survivors of his family. Ships deliver cannon, powder and supplies but after eight months hunger and disease win the day.

In 1409 Harlech Castle falls to the English.

During the terrible siege Edmund Mortimer, alongside so many, died of disease but Owain is able to make good a daring escape and rally the failing cause. He must pay a heavy personal price however, and leave behind his beloved wife, two daughters and their children, plus his son, Lionel and his three daughters, to the mercy of the English. All are captured and taken to the Tower of London.

Overcoming such personal loss, Owain leads a raid of old, deep into Shropshire, but the Marcher Lords are ready and waiting. Rhys the Black, Philip Scudmore and Rhys ap Tudwr are all captured and executed. No longer a threat and lacking support, Owain can only seek refuge in the wild mountains of Snowdonia, as his forebears had done, where he continues to hold out with his loyal band of followers.

Then, in the year of 1413, Owain Glyndŵr disappears.

The Welsh Seers can only compare Owain's disappearance to that of Arthur, who is said to have vanished into the mists of Avalon and, like the legendary Arthur, Owain Glyndŵr, the last Native Prince of Wales to rise against the English, sleeps to awaken at the call of his people.

In reality, Owain, shattered and now an old man, had secretly retired from his mighty efforts to his daughter's house in Herefordshire, never to be heard of again, never to accept a King's pardon.

This Welsh Prince may not have fulfilled an ancient prophecy but Owain Glyndŵr had led Wales to become an independent nation, something the people would always remember, a national spirit identified with, and one which the passing centuries would aspire to.

King Henry IV had triumphed over all of his enemies but the effort had broken him. Suffering from his heart and epilepsy it was clear he could rule no more. Then, upon his death, in the same year as Owain's disappearance, his son succeeds to the throne as King Henry V.

Yet, the prophecies were still to be fulfilled, that a King of Celtic decent would one day rule both England and Wales, though few must believe such an occurrence could rise from the ashes. For its conclusion, attention must now turn to the Tudwr family who had stormed Conwy Castle and fought and died beside Owain throughout.

Of the four Tudwr brothers, only Maredudd had escaped but the new King is chivalrous to the vanquished Welsh. He does not press Wales but recruits them into his armies to make war on France, for this King intended to win back lands on the continent and claim the French throne.

Once such Welshman seeking employment is Maredudd's son, named Owain, who gains the remarkable position of Page to King Henry V. He is made to anglicise his name and chooses Tudor, then travels with the King to Normandy where Henry's fearless and capable leadership defeats the Flower of France at Agincourt. For his gallantry on this field, Owain Tudor is promoted to Squire to the body of the King.

Henry V, however, was not destined to become a King of France and while on campaign there in 1422 dies of dysentery leaving his son to become the boy King Henry VI and his Queen, Katherine of Valois, a widow at the age of twenty. A Regent is appointed until the boy King comes of age but the wars do not go well in France and soon Joan of Arc would renew French victories.

Upon Henry V's death, Owain Tudor remained in Royal service as Clerk of the Wardrobe to the Queen who is forced to stay in England because of her child, Henry VI. With the boy King in the care of the Regent she finds herself left to her own devices and about to break all the rules of Royal etiquette.

Katherine falls in love with the charming Owain. They marry in secret and live together for eleven happy years, raising five children, but the two most important would be Edmund and Jasper. Then, in 1436, the marriage is discovered and the Queen sent to Bormersdey Abbey where she dies within a year. Owain seeks sanctuary but is arrested and sent to Newgate Prison. He escapes to his family's old estates in Anglesey where he remains until his stepson, the young King, comes of age.

Meanwhile, with only Calais remaining under English rule, the long, drawn out, 'Hundred Years War,' with France was coming to an end, but with the returning armies the balance of power in England would result in yet another conflict.

Now of age, King Henry VI looks kindly upon his stepfather and half brothers and grants Edmund the Earldom of Richmond and Jasper the Earldom of Pembroke. In the approaching conflict they would repay Henry's generosity by proving their unswerving loyalty to the Lancastrian cause against the Yorkists.

This new King, however, was also causing many to be discontent, none more so than Richard, Duke of York, whose exclusion from court leads to an inevitable confrontation with the Lancastrian King when, in 1455, a battle at St. Albans begins a series of struggles to gain power, a struggle to be named, the 'Wars of the Roses.'

Of the Tudor's, Edmund married Lady Margaret Beaufort, the great, great granddaughter of Edward III, but in the ensuing conflict he is captured and dies a prisoner in Carmarthen Castle. His thirteen year old bride though is already pregnant and Jasper takes her to the safety of Pembroke Castle where, on 28th January 1457, a boy child is born and she names him Henry Tudor.

As the power struggle swings between the red rose of Lancaster and the white rose of York, both England and Wales split with division between these two warring Houses. The south and west of Wales followed Jasper and his father, Owain, while the borders supported the Mortimer's.

Upon Richard Mortimer's death at the battle of Wakefield, his nineteen year old son, Edward, Earl of March and now Duke of York, was about to succeed his father's claim to the throne. He rides out to meet the Lancastrians at Mortimer's Cross where, on a cold February morning in 1461, the two armies clash. Four thousand and five hundred lay dead but Edward had beaten the Lancastrian force and won the Crown of England to become King Edward IV.

During the battle Owain Tudor is captured then later beheaded at Hereford. His last words, 'that head shall be on the block that was want to lie on Queen Katherine's lap.' Jasper, however, escapes and, with the young Henry Tudor, flees to Brittany where the French King gives them refuge.

In England, and after nine years, the Red Rose of Henry VI is briefly restored until he is again beaten at Tewkesbury. This time Edward IV kills all surviving opponents to the throne and is able to rule without challenge until his unexpected death of a severe cold in 1483.

The King's brother, Richard of Gloucester, is appointed protector of his twelve year old nephew who was to be crowned, Edward V, but the boy and his brother are declared illegitimate and disappear within the Tower of London.

Richard's ruthless coup shatters the Yorkist regime and gains him the Throne of England as King Richard III. Those Yorkists forced into exile gather at the 'Court' of Henry Tudor, a young man who had possessed little hope of ever making good a distant claim to the Lancastrian throne but now found himself the attention of many voices urging him to oppose Richard.

Henry Tudor would come to represent both the House of Lancaster and York when, on Christmas Day 1484, he swears an oath to defeat King Richard, secure the throne and marry Elizabeth of York, daughter of the late Edward IV, to create peace.

True to his word, in August 1485, Henry, now aged twenty eight years old, lands near Milford Haven in south Wales with an army of two thousand French mercenaries funded by the King of France. On their march through Wales they are joined by a formidable Welsh army, led by Rhys ap Thomas, and continue through Shrewsbury into the Midlands of England.

King Richard had placed himself at Nottingham close to his northern supporters and in a central position to act against any opponents. Then, upon hearing of the invasion marches south with a mighty army ten thousand strong to meet Henry Tudor.

Experienced and capable in battle, Richard arrays his force on a hill near Market Bosworth and prepares to confront his enemy. His supporters, concerned at the lack of many noble loyalties, advise him to leave the field but Richard retorts, 'This day will I die as a King or win.' Henry Tudor was also seeking support from

English families, including the very powerful Stanley's who had marched with five thousand men to the battle but with Stanley's son held hostage by King Richard there could be no certainty as to which side he would join.

Then, on 22nd day of August the two armies advance. The fighting is bitter and hazy with the stench of gun powder from small cannons. The heavily armoured men are soon exhausted and reinforcements are called up but King Richard's show reluctance and Stanley still held back.

Suddenly the King spies Henry Tudor moving across to confer with the Stanley's and charges down the hill straight for him. While cutting through Henry's entourage, Richard III, King of England, is pulled from his horse and hacked to pieces. Upon the King's death, Stanley advances on the Royal army and decides the day.

Henry Tudor is victorious.

The Lord Stanley then retrieves the crown from a bush where it had fallen and places it upon the head of the Earl of Richmond, Henry Tudor. A King of native origin and blood.

This claim to the throne however was poor and he would have to prove himself a worthy successor or face condemnation. Henry was also fully aware of the importance attached to the fulfilment of bardic prophecies.

The Wars of the Roses now left a huge gap in the ruling Gentry and so the new Tudor dynasty began sweeping changes. King Henry VII offers much needed peace both amongst the English Barons and with Wales. He marries Princess Elizabeth, the heiress of York, so merging these warring Houses and their Red There will come of course many more struggles and many more and White symbols into the Tudor rose. Welshmen are elevated into government and welcomed in court. He opens trade and even more heartening withdraws the Marcher Lords' power with new laws forbidding private armies.

During their harmonious reign they raise seven children but only three would outlive their mother. While the country, which had been ruled by the same feudal system since the Norman Conquest, now begins to change.

Then in 1489 he proclaims his eldest son and heir, named Arthur in honour of the legendary leader and contender of an ancient prophecy, as Prince of Wales.

The young Prince possessed the hopes of his father and is married at the age of fifteen to Katherine of Aragon but she is soon alone in a foreign country after her new husband dies during an influenza epidemic.

When laid to rest in Westminster Abbey, in 1509, Henry Tudor is watched over by a stone dragon, a King's recognition of his Celtic decent who had ruled both Wales and England. The next son in line to the throne is named after his father. The realm passes to King Henry VIII and he would continue his father's work building a Royal Navy to rule the seas but his actions would also divide his land and see the beginning of the religious wars. Britain's evolution was about to take on a new dimension.

Only each individual however can judge if an ancient prophecy had been fulfilled; but it is a fine ending to those words that for over a Millennium had inspired a people, and it is a fine beginning, for the Tudor dynasty would influence the shaping of the World.

centuries to pass before the like of Owain Glyndŵr's Parliament could be seen again, but with such words at least hope can be kept alive. For, by remembering in whose footsteps we pass, our appreciation and respect will be all the greater.

Post Script

****

On the 18th day of September, in the year of our Lord, 1997, the vote for a Welsh Assembly was cast. Perhaps a new era in the recognition of Wales' identity, culture, and unique language.

****

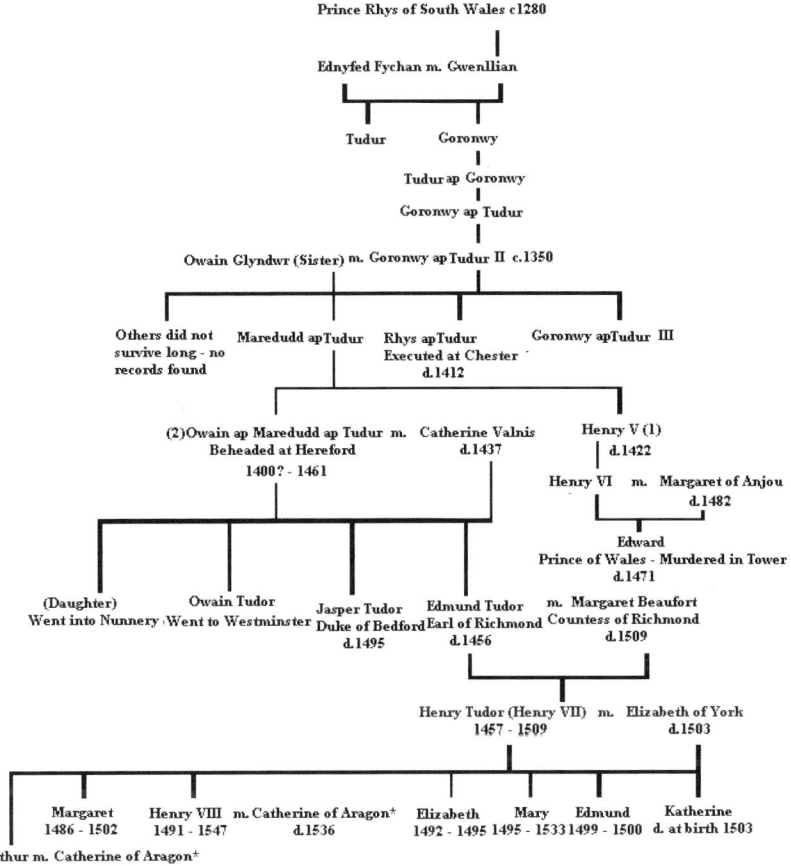